Bobbie Matela, Managing Editor
Carol Wilson Mansfield, Art Director
Mary Ann Frits, Editorial Director
Sandy Scoville, Pattern Editor
Kelly Robinson and Kathy Wesley, Editorial Staff
Kathryn Smith, Assistant Editor
Graphic Solutions inc-chgo, Book Design

MW01054317

INTRODUCTION

Everyone knows that when your feet feel good, you feel good all over. And what better way to pamper them than with soft, cozy socks?

Cute as a bug, and snug as a bug in a rug, each of these socks is designed to warm hearts as well as soles!

Our detailed instructions guide you through sock-knitting basics, and designer Edie Eckman presents a dozen imaginative anklet and cuffed sock styles, all worked in sport-weight wool.

From the just-for-giggles ringlets of *Curl Your Toes*, to the tender-as-butter softness of *This Little Pinky...*, these socks are fanciful, classic, stylish, and fun—to make, to give, and to wear.

Learn to Knit Socks is published by DRG, 306 East Parr Road, Berne, IN 46711. Printed in USA. All rights reserved. This publication may not be reproduced in part or in whole without written permission from the publisher.

RETAIL STORES: If you would like to carry this pattern book or any other DRG publications, visit DRGwholesale.com

Every effort has been made to ensure that the instructions in this publication are complete and accurate. We cannot, however, take responsibility for human error, typographical mistakes or variations in individual work. Please visit AnniesCustomerCare.com to check for pattern updates.

ISBN: 978-0-88195-871-3

34 35 36 37 38 39 40

ABBREVIATIONS AND SYMBOLS

beg . . . . begin(ning)

bl(s) . . . . back loop(s)

inc . . . . increase

K . . . . knit

P . . . . purl

patt . . . . pattern

PSSO . . . . pass slipped stitch over

rem . . . . remain(ing)

rep . . . . repeat(ing)

rnd(s) . . . . round(s)

sk . . . . skip

sl . . . . slip

sl st(s) . . . . slip stitch(es)

SSK . . . . slip, slip, knit

st(s) . . . . stitch(es)

tog . . . . together

yb . . . . yarn back

yf . . . . yarn forward

YO . . . . yarn over

* An asterisk is used to mark the beginning of a portion of instructions to be worked more than once; thus, "rep from * twice more" means after working the instructions once, repeat the instructions following the asterisk twice more (3 times in all).

—The number after a long dash at the end of a row indicates the number of stitches you should have when the row has been completed.

( ) Parentheses are used to enclose instructions which should be worked the exact number of times specified immediately following the parentheses, such as (K2, P2) twice.

( ) Parentheses are also used to provide additional information to clarify instructions.

METRIC CONVERSION CHART

KNITTING NEEDLES CONVERSION CHART

U.S.	0	1		2		3	4	5		6	7	8	9	10	10½			11	13	15
Metric(mm)	2	2¼	2½	2¾	3	3⅛	3½	3¾	4	4¼	4½	5	5¼	5¾	6½	7	7½	8	9	10

SOCKS

Socks are fun to knit and fun to wear — and hand-knitted ones are at the peak of fashion. If you're a knitter who has never made socks before, we have some hints to make your project easier.

Choose the right yarn...

Remember that socks need to be comfortable — and that means they should be made of yarn that includes at least some wool — that wonderful, soft fiber that absorbs moisture and molds itself to the foot shape. A 100% acrylic yarn will leave feet hot and damp, and 100% cotton yarn doesn't have enough stretch for a comfortable fit.

A part-wool or all-wool yarn makes wonderful socks. We made all of our models in Spinrite® Berella® Country Garden D.K. This Claire Murray Collection of 100% Merino wool is machine washable. However, you can use any similar yarn in sport or DK weight.

Make the correct size...

Big feet, small feet, wide feet, skinny feet — how do you choose the correct size for each?

Fortunately, the stretchability of wool means that for most feet, you need only adjust the length of the sole. The best way to judge is to have the person who is to wear the sock stand barefoot on a flat surface while you measure the foot length from back of heel to end of longest toe. If you can't measure an actual foot, ask the recipient-to-be for her shoe size.

These are the average measurements for women's shoe sizes to use as a guide for sizing your socks.

Shoe Size	Foot Measurement	Sock Length
5-5$\frac{1}{2}$	8$\frac{3}{4}$"	8$\frac{1}{4}$"
6-6$\frac{1}{2}$	9"	8$\frac{3}{4}$"
7-7$\frac{1}{2}$	9$\frac{3}{8}$"	9"
8-8$\frac{1}{2}$	9$\frac{3}{4}$"	9$\frac{1}{4}$"
9-9$\frac{1}{2}$	10"	9$\frac{3}{4}$"
10-10$\frac{1}{2}$	10$\frac{3}{8}$"	10"

The yarn amounts specified in our patterns are based on a women's shoe size 7-8. If you are making a longer sock, you will need to purchase additional yarn.

Anatomy of a sock... (Fig 1)

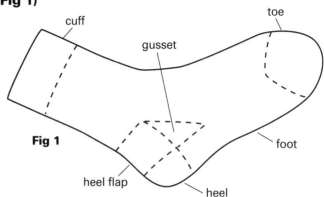

Fig 1

We know you hate the word "gauge"...

But if you don't take time to check your gauge, the sock will not fit. All the socks are knitted to a stitch gauge of 7 sts = 1" when worked in stockinette stitch (knit 1 row, purl 1 row). But at least you don't have to worry about row gauge when knitting socks!

We suggest Size 3 needles — but you should use whatever size gives you the specified gauge.

Round and round we go...

With one exception, all of our socks are knitted in the round on a set of four double-pointed needles. This avoids sewn seams and makes the sock more comfortable to wear.

The exception is the argyle sock, in which the argyle design part is worked in turned rows.

When working with four needles in the round, the stitches are divided onto three needles, and the fourth is used to make the stitches (Fig 2).

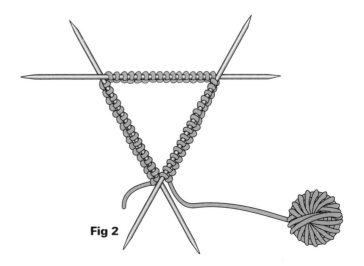

Fig 2

Cast on for elasticity...

A beautiful hand-knitted sock doesn't do the wearer much good if the cast-on edge of the cuff is too tight to go over the foot! So since all of our socks are worked from the cuff down, you need to use a cast-on method that gives a lot of stretch. This is the method we used for our socks:

All necessary stitches are cast on to one needle, then separated onto three needles as instructed in the patterns.

To begin, make a slip knot and place the loop on the needle in your right hand, leaving a long strand. For these socks you will need a 36" strand.

Step 1:

Place the thumb and index finger of your left hand between the long strand and the strand coming from the skein of yarn; close your other three fingers over the strands to hold them against your palm. Spread your thumb and index fingers apart and draw the yarn into a V **(Fig 3)**.

Fig 3

Step 2:

Place the needle in front of the strand around your thumb and bring it underneath this strand; carry needle over and under the strand on your index finger **(Fig 4)**; draw through loop on thumb **(Fig 5)**.

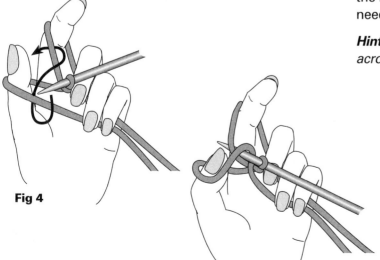

Fig 4

Fig 5

Step 3:

Drop the loop from your thumb and draw up the strand to form a stitch on the needle.

Repeat Steps 1 through 3 until you have cast on the number of stitches indicated in the pattern. Remember to count the beginning slip knot as a stitch.

Hint: Your cast-on stitches must be loose so the sock will stretch when pulled over your foot. The stitches should move easily on the needle. If you tend to cast on tightly, use a larger size needle, or cast on using two needles held together.

Knitting with four needles...

On the first row, join the work divided on the three needles by inserting the fourth (free) needle into the first stitch on the first needle **(Fig 6)**.

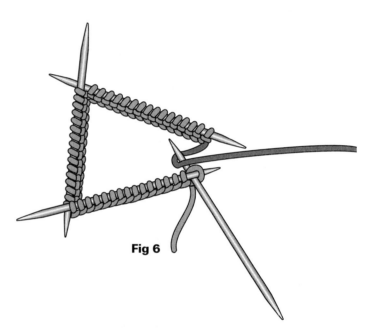

Fig 6

When the stitches on the first needle are worked, use the now free needle to work the stitches on the next needle; repeat on the third needle.

Hint: To avoid gaps between needles, pull yarn tightly across to the first stitch of each new needle.

Turning the heel...

Since a foot is at an angle to the leg, socks must be shaped the same way. To do this, we use a series of decrease rows after the heel flap is worked to change the direction of the work. This is fun to do, and is called turning a heel.

For example:

If you are working with 48 sts, place 24 sts on the heel needle and 24 sts on a stitch holder. These sts on the stitch holder are left unworked while a heel flap is worked on the 24 sts. Work straight for the number of inches specified in the pattern (**Fig 7**).

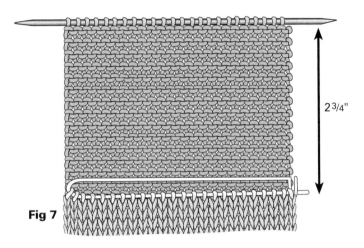

Fig 7

2 3/4"

Then work 10 decrease rows. You have 14 sts on the needle. Turning the heel has been completed. Now you will pick up sts to work the gusset.

Picking up stitches...

After turning the heel in a sock pattern, it is necessary to pick up sts along both sides of the heel flap. When working with sport weight yarn, picking up sts is best done with a size F (**3.75mm**) crochet hook, then slipping the stitches from it to the knitting needle. (A knitting needle may be used instead of the crochet hook.)

To pick up a stitch, hold the knitting with its right side facing you. Hold yarn from the skein in your left hand, behind the work, and hold the crochet hook in your right hand. Insert hook into work from front to back, one stitch (**at least 2 threads**) from the edge (**Fig 8**);

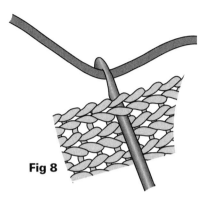

Fig 8

hook yarn and pull a loop back through work, making one stitch on hook (**Fig 9**).

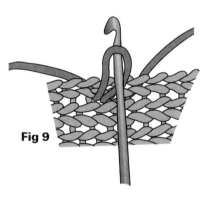

Fig 9

Now slip stitch off crochet hook and onto knitting needle, being sure to have the stitch in the correct position, without twisting it (**Fig 10**).

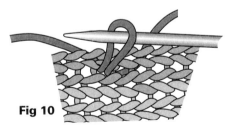

Fig 10

The specific pattern will indicate the exact number of stitches to pick up along each side of the heel flap. Follow pattern to complete sock.

SPECIAL TECHNIQUES

Weaving on two needles—Kitchener Stitch...
This method of weaving is used for the toes of the socks.

To weave the edges together and form an unbroken line of stockinette stitch, divide all stitches evenly onto two knitting needles - one behind the other.

Thread yarn into tapestry needle; with wrong sides together, work from right to left as follows:

Step 1:
Insert tapestry needle into the first stitch on the front needle as to purl **(Fig 1)**. Draw yarn through stitch, leaving stitch on knitting needle.

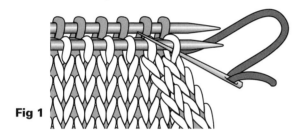

Fig 1

Step 2:
Insert tapestry needle into the first stitch on back needle as to knit **(Fig 2)**, leaving stitch on knitting needle.

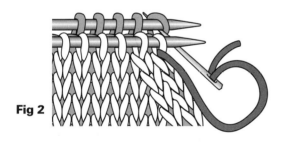

Fig 2

Step 3:
Insert tapestry needle into the first stitch on the front needle as to knit. Slip stitch off knitting needle. Insert tapestry needle into the next stitch on same (front) needle as to purl **(Fig 3)**. Draw yarn through stitches, leaving stitch on knitting needle.

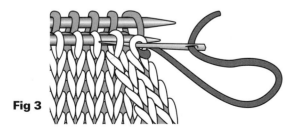

Fig 3

Step 4:
Insert tapestry needle into the first stitch on back needle as to purl **(Fig 4)**. Draw yarn through stitch and slip stitch off knitting needle. Insert needle into the next stitch on back needle as to knit, leaving stitch on knitting needle.

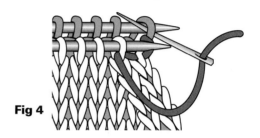

Fig 4

Repeat Steps 3 and 4 until all stitches on both needles have been woven together.

Finish off and weave in end.

Hint: When weaving, do not pull yarn tightly or too loosely; woven stitches should be the same size as adjacent knitted stitches.

Working With Charts...
The charts in this book are used when knitting with more than one color per row.

When working in rows, read odd numbered rows from right to left, and even numbered rows from left to right.

Odd numbered rows represent the right side of your work, and are usually knit. Even numbered rows represent the wrong side of your work, and are usually purled.

When working in rounds, every row on the chart is a right side row, and are always read from right to left.

Duplicate Stitch...
Duplicate stitch is an embroidery stitch that duplicates the "V" of the knit stitch it will cover. Duplicate stitch is often used when carrying yarns is not practical.

As in the case of the Yours, Mine and Argyles pattern on page 22, white diagonal lines are created with duplicate stitch after the sock is completed.

To work duplicate stitch, thread a 24" length of yarn in color stated through a tapestry needle. Find location of first stitch (marked by an arrow on the chart) by reading diagonal lines on chart. On wrong side of sock, anchor thread by weaving the yarn away from and back toward location of the first stitch.

Bring needle up at base of first stitch and slide needle under both loops of stitch above **(Fig 5)**; insert needle down in same space at base of stitch **(Fig 6)**.

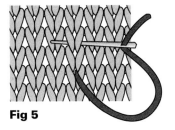 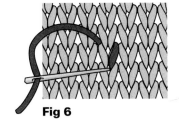

Fig 5   **Fig 6**

Following chart, repeat for remaining stitches, working upward diagonally. When last duplicate stitch is completed, weave through several stitches in both directions on wrong side to anchor thread.

Begin each diagonal line with a new strand of yarn.

KNITTING REVIEW

Knit - K:

Insert right needle in stitch from front to back under the left needle;

bring yarn from skein under and over point of right needle;

draw yarn through stitch with right needle point;

slip stitch off left needle. New stitch is on right needle.

Purl - P:

Insert right needle in stitch from right to left in front of left needle;

holding yarn in front, bring yarn from skein around right needle counterclockwise;

with right needle, draw yarn back through stitch;

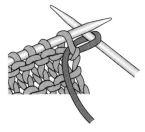

slip stitch off left needle. New stitch is on right needle.

BASIC SOCK

Materials:

Berella® Country Garden D.K. sport weight wool yarn, 3.5 oz (270 yds, 100 g) Delphinium #32

Size 3 (3.25mm) 7" double-pointed knitting needles, or size required for gauge

Size F (3.75mm) crochet hook (optional for picking up sts)

Stitch marker

2¹/₂" long stitch holder

Size 18 tapestry needle

Gauge:

7 sts = 1" in stockinette stitch (knit one row, purl one row)

Special Abbreviation

Slip, Slip, Knit (SSK):
Sl next 2 sts, one at a time, as to knit; insert left-hand needle through both sts from right to left; K2 tog— SSK made.

Instructions

Sock (make 2)
Loosely cast on 48 sts onto one needle (see cast-on instructions on page 4).

Divide evenly onto 3 needles, being careful not to twist sts. Mark beg of rnds.

Cuff:
Rnds 1 through 4:
Keeping the sts separated on 3 needles, knit all sts.

Rnds 5 through 18:
* K1, P1; rep from * around.

Rnds 19 through 28:
Knit.

Heel:
Now it's time to begin the heel, and the stitches need to be rearranged on the needles.

Sl the last 12 sts of Rnd 28 onto free needle; knit first 12 sts of Rnd 28 onto same needle: these 24 sts make the heel flap; slip the remaining 24 sts onto stitch holder for instep to be worked later.

Turn work: you will now work in rows.

HEEL FLAP:
Row 1 (wrong side):
Sl 1 as to purl, purl across row. Turn.

Row 2 (right side):
Sl 1 as to knit, knit across row. Turn.

Rep Rows 1 and 2 until heel flap measures 2³/₄", ending by working a right side row.

Turning Heel:
Row 1 (wrong side):
P14, P2 tog; P1. Turn, leaving rem 7 sts unworked.

Row 2 (right side):
Sl 1 as to knit, K5, SSK (see Special Abbreviation), K1. Turn, leaving rem 7 sts unworked.

Row 3:
Sl 1 as to purl, P6, P2 tog; P1. Turn, leaving rem 5 sts unworked.

Row 4:
Sl 1 as to knit, K7, SSK, K1. Turn, leaving rem 5 sts unworked.

Row 5:
Sl 1 as to purl, P8, P2 tog; P1. Turn, leaving rem 3 sts unworked.

Row 6:
Sl 1 as to knit, K9, SSK, K1. Turn, leaving rem 3 sts unworked.

Row 7:
Sl 1 as to purl, P10, P2 tog; P1. Turn, leaving rem st unworked.

Row 8:
Sl 1 as to knit, K11, SSK, K1. Turn, leaving rem st unworked.

Row 9:
Sl 1 as to purl, P12, P2 tog. Turn.

Row 10:
Sl 1 as to knit, K12, SSK—14 sts.

Gusset:
With right side of heel flap facing you, with crochet hook (or free needle), pick up and slip onto free needle 13 sts along left side of heel flap; on second free needle, knit 24 instep sts from stitch holder; with crochet hook (or free needle), pick up and slip onto third free needle 13 sts along right side of heel flap; knit first 7 sts of heel flap onto same needle. Sl rem 7 sts of heel flap onto beg of first needle—64 sts.

Rnd 1:
On first needle, knit to last 3 sts; K2 tog; K1; on second needle, K24; on third needle, K1, SSK, knit rem sts.

Rnd 2:
Knit.

Rep Rnds 1 and 2 seven times—48 sts.

Foot:
Work even until foot measures about 2" shorter than desired length of sock (see "Make the correct size..." on page 3).

Toe Shaping:
Rnd 1:
On first needle, knit to last 3 sts; K2 tog; K1; on second needle, K1, SSK, knit to last 3 sts; K2 tog; K1; on third needle, K1, SSK, knit rem sts.

Rnd 2:
Knit.

Rnds 3 through 12:
Rep Rnds 1 and 2. At end of Rnd 12—24 sts.

Rnds 13 and 14:
Rep Rnd 1. At end of Rnd 14—16 sts.

Knit sts from first needle onto third needle.

Cut yarn, leaving a 12" end for weaving.

Finishing
With tapestry needle, weave toe together (see Special Techniques on page 6). Weave in all ends.

FAIR PAIR

Materials:
Berella® Country Garden D.K. sport weight wool yarn,
   3.5 oz (270 yds, 100 g) Bisque #45; 1.75 oz
   (135 yds, 50 g) Lilac Heather #81
Size 3 (3.25mm) 7" double-pointed knitting needles,
   or size required for gauge
Size F (3.75mm) crochet hook (optional for picking
   up sts)
Stitch marker
2¹⁄₂" long stitch holder
Size 18 tapestry needle

Gauge:
7 sts = 1" in stockinette stitch (knit one row,
   purl one row)

Instructions

Sock (make 2)
Note: See page 6 for instructions on reading charts.

With Bisque, cast on 48 sts.

Divide evenly onto 3 needles, being careful
not to twist sts. Mark beg of rnds.

Cuff:
Rnd 1:
* K2, P2; rep from
* around.

Rnds 2 through 15:
Rep Rnd 1.

Calf:
Work Rnds 1 through
44 from chart, read-
ing every rnd from
right to left.

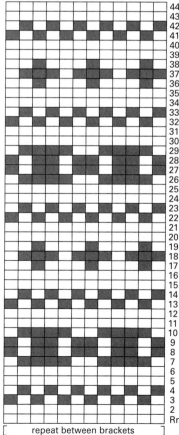

Bisque

Lilac Heather

repeat between brackets

Rnd 1 ← Start here

Heel:
Sl last 12 sts of last rnd onto
free needle; K12 onto same needle;
sl rem 24 sts onto stitch holder for instep. Turn.

HEEL FLAP:
Row 1 (wrong side):
Sl 1 as to purl, purl across. Turn.

Row 2:
Sl 1 as to knit; * K1, sl 1 as to purl; rep from * 22 times
more; K1.

Rep Rnds 1 and 2 until heel flap measures 2³⁄₄", ending
on a right side row.

Turning Heel, Gusset, Foot, and Toe Shaping:
Work same as for Basic Sock beg on page 8.

Finishing
See Finishing for Basic Sock on page 9.

CURL YOUR TOES

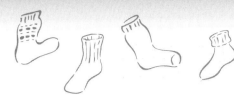

Materials:

Berella® Country Garden D.K. sport weight wool yarn, 3.5 oz (270 yds, 100 g) each, Wild Violet #28 and Sea Green #38

Size 3 (3.25mm) 7" double-pointed knitting needles, or size required for gauge

Size F (3.75mm) crochet hook (optional for picking up sts)

Stitch marker

2¹/₂" long stitch holder

Size 18 tapestry needle

Gauge:

7 sts = 1" in stockinette stitch (knit one row, purl one row)

Instructions

Sock (make 2)

With Sea Green, cast on 48 sts.

Divide evenly onto 3 needles, being careful not to twist sts. Mark beg of rnds.

Cuff:
Rnd 1:
* K2, P2; rep from * around.

Rep Rnd 1 until cuff measures 5".

Ankle:
Rnds 1 through 10:
With Wild Violet, knit.

Heel:
Sl last 12 sts of last rnd onto free needle; K12 onto same needle; sl rem 24 sts onto stitch holder for instep. Turn.

HEEL FLAP:
Row 1 (wrong side):
Sl 1 as to purl, purl across. Turn.

Row 2 (right side):
Sl 1 as to knit; * K1, sl 1 as to purl; rep from * 10 times more; K1.

Rep Rnds 1 and 2 until heel flap measures 2³/₄", ending on a right side row.

Turning Heel, Gusset and Foot:
With Wild Violet, work same as for Basic Sock beg on page 8.

Toe Shaping:
With Sea Green, work same as for Basic Sock on page 9.

Curlicues (make 6)
With Sea Green, cast on 38 sts.

K2 tog; * K2 tog; sl first st over 2nd st; rep from * across; bind off last st. Cut yarn, leaving a 6" end.

Finishing

Step 1:
With tapestry needle, weave toe together (see Special Techniques on page 6). Weave in all ends.

Step 2:
Turn down cuff and tack curlicues evenly spaced around cast-on edge of cuff.

FOOTSIE-CUFFS

Materials:
Berella® Country Garden D.K. sport weight wool yarn,
3.5 oz (270 yds, 100 g) Grey Heather #73; 1.75 oz (135
yds, 50 g) each, Primose #7 and Wild Violet #28
Size 3 (3.25mm) 7" double-pointed knitting needles,
or size required for gauge
Size F (3.75mm) crochet hook (optional for picking
up sts)
Stitch marker
2¹/₂" stitch holder
Size 18 tapestry needle

Gauge:
7 sts = 1" in stockinette stitch (knit one row,
purl one row)

Instructions

Sock (make 2)
With Grey Heather, cast on 48 sts.

Divide evenly onto 3 needles, being careful not to twist
sts. Mark beg of rnds.

Cuff:
Rnd 1 (right side):
* K1, P1; rep from * around.

Rnd 2:
Rep Rnd 1.

Rnd 3:
Knit.

Rnd 4:
With Wild Violet, * K3, sl 1 as to purl; rep from
* 11 times more.

Rnd 5:
* P3, yb, sl 1 as to purl, yf; rep from * 11 times more.

Rnd 6:
With Primose, K1; * sl 1 as to purl, K3; rep from
* 10 times more; sl 1 as to purl, K2.

Rnd 7:
P1; * yb, sl 1 as to purl, yf, P3; rep from * 10 times more;
yb, sl 1 as to purl, yf, P2.

Rnd 8:
With Grey Heather, * K3, sl 1 as to purl; rep from
* 11 times more.

Rnd 9:
* P3, yb, sl 1 as to purl, yf; rep from * 11 times more.

Rnd 10:
With Wild Violet, K1; * sl 1 as to purl, K3; rep from
* 10 times more; sl 1 as to purl, K2.

Rnd 11:
P1; * yb, sl 1 as to purl, yf, P3; rep from * 10 times
more; sl 1 as to purl, K2.

Rnd 12:
With Primose, * K3, sl 1 as to purl; rep from * 11 times
more.

Rnd 13:
* P3, yb, sl 1 as to purl, yf; rep from * 11 times more.

Rnd 14:
With Grey Heather, K1; * sl 1 as to purl, K3; rep from
* 10 times more; sl 1 as to purl, K2.

Rnd 15:
P1; * yb, sl 1 as to purl, P3; rep from * 10 times more; yb, sl 1 as to purl, P2.

Rnds 16 through 27:
Rep Rnds 4 through 13.

Rnds 28 and 29:
With Grey Heather, knit.

Rnd 30 (turning ridge):
Purl.

Ankle:
Rnd 1:
Knit.

Rnd 2:
* K1, P1; rep from * 11 times more.

Rep Rnd 2 until ankle measures 2$\frac{1}{2}$" from turning ridge.

Next Rnd:
Yf, sl 1 as to purl, yb, sl this st back to left-hand needle; turn; yb, knit around.

Note: The direction of your knitting has been changed. Turn the sock inside out and fold the cuff down allowing the right side to show.

Heel:
Sl last 12 sts of last rnd onto free needle; K12 onto same needle; sl rem 24 sts onto stitch holder for instep. Turn.

HEEL FLAP:
Row 1 (wrong side):
Sl 1 as to purl, purl across. Turn.

Row 2 (right side):
Sl 1 as to knit, knit across. Turn.

Row 3:
With Primose, sl 1 as to purl, purl across. Turn.

Row 4:
Sl 1 as to knit, knit across. Turn.

Rep Rows 1 through 4 until heel flap measures 2$\frac{3}{4}$", ending by working a right side row.

Turning Heel, Gusset, Foot, and Toe Shaping:
With Grey Heather, work same as for Basic Sock beg on page 8.

Finishing
See Finishing for Basic Sock on page 9.

FRECKLED FOOTSIES

Materials:
Berella® Country Garden D.K. sport weight wool yarn,
   3.5 oz (270 yds, 100 g) Shrimp #14; 1.75 oz
   (135 yds, 50 g) Snowdrop #1
Size 3 (3.25mm) 7" double-pointed knitting needles, or
   size required for gauge
Size F (3.75mm) crochet hook (optional for picking
   up sts)
Stitch marker
2¹/₂" stitch holder
Size 18 tapestry needle

Gauge:
7 sts = 1" in stockinette stitch (knit every rnd)

Instructions

Sock (make 2)
With Shrimp, cast on 48 sts.

Divide evenly onto 3 needles, being careful not to
twist sts. Mark beg of rnds.

Ribbing:
Rnd 1 (right side):
* K1, P1; rep from * around.

Rnds 2 through 11:
Rep Rnd 1.

Ankle:
Rnd 1:
With Snowdrop, * K1, sl 3 as to purl; rep from * around.

Rnd 2:
* P1, yb, sl 3 as to purl, yf; rep from * around.

Rnds 3 and 4:
With Shrimp, knit.

Rnd 5:
With Snowdrop, sl 2 as to purl; * K1, sl 3 as to purl; rep
from * 10 times more; K1, sl 1 as to purl.

Rnd 6:
Sl 2 as to purl; * yf, P1, yb, sl 3 as to purl; rep from
* 10 times more; yf, P1, yb, sl 1 as to purl.

Rnds 7 and 8:
With Shrimp, knit.

Rnds 9 through 64:
Rep Rnds 1 through 8 seven times more.

Heel:
Sl last 12 sts of last rnd onto free needle; K12 from
same needle; sl rem 24 sts onto stitch holder for
instep. Turn.

HEEL FLAP:
Row 1 (wrong side):
Sl 1 as to purl, purl across. Turn.

Row 2 (right side):
Sl 1 as to knit; * K1, sl 1 as to purl; rep from * 10 times
more; K1.

Rep Rows 1 and 2 until heel flap measures 2³/₄", ending
on a right side row.

Turning Heel, Gusset, Foot, and Toe Shaping:
Work same as for Basic Sock beg on page 8.

Finishing
See Finishing for Basic Sock on page 9.

HEART AND SOLE

Materials:
Berella® Country Garden D.K. sport weight wool yarn, 3.5 oz (270 yds, 100 g) Brick Red #22; 1.75 oz (135 yds, 50 g) Snowdrop #1
Size 3 (3.25mm) 7" double-pointed knitting needles, or size required for gauge
Size F (3.75mm) crochet hook (optional for picking up sts)
Stitch marker
2¹/₂" long stitch holder
Size 18 tapestry needle

Gauge:
7 sts = 1" in stockinette stitch (knit one row, purl one row)

Pattern Stitch
Bobble:
In st indicated work (K1, YO, K1, YO, K1); turn; sl 1 as to purl, P4; turn; sl 1 as to knit, K4; turn; sl 1 as to purl, (P2 tog) twice; turn; sl 1, K2 tog, PSSO—bobble made.

Instructions

Sock (make 2)
With Snowdrop, cast on 48 sts.

Divide evenly onto 3 needles, being careful not to twist sts. Mark beg of rnds.

Cuff:
Rnd 1 (right side):
Knit.

Rnd 2:
P2, bobble in next st (see Pattern Stitch); * P5, bobble; rep from * 6 times more; P3—8 bobbles.

Rnd 3:
P2, K1; * P5, K1; rep from * 6 times more; P3.

Rnds 4 through 17:
Rep Rnd 3.

Rnd 18:
Rep Rnd 2.

Rnd 19:
Knit.

Ankle Ribbing:
Rnd 1:
With Brick Red, knit.

Rnd 2:
* K1, P1; rep from * around.

Rep Rnd 2 until ankle ribbing measures 2¹/₄".

Next Rnd:
Yf, sl 1 as to purl, yb, sl this st back to left-hand needle; turn; yb, knit around.

Note: The direction of your knitting has been changed. Turn the sock inside out and fold the cuff down allowing the right side to show.

Knit 8 rnds.

Heel:
Sl last 12 sts of last rnd onto free needle; K12 onto same needle; sl rem 24 sts onto stitch holder for instep. Turn.

HEEL FLAP:
Row 1 (wrong side):
Sl 1 as to purl, purl across. Turn.

Row 2 (right side):
Sl 1 as to knit; * K1, sl 1 as to purl; rep from * 10 times more; K1.

Rep Rows 1 and 2 until heel flap measures 2³/₄", ending on a right side row.

Turning Heel, Gusset, Foot, and Toe Shaping:
Work same as for Basic Sock beg on page 8.

Finishing
See Finishing for Basic Sock on page 9.

PERI-TWINKLE TOES

Materials:
Berella® Country Garden D.K. sport weight wool yarn,
  3.5 oz (270 yds, 100 g) Wild Violet #28
Size 3 (3.25mm) 7" double-pointed knitting needles,
  or size required for gauge
Size F (3.75mm) crochet hook (optional for picking
  up sts)
Stitch marker
2¹/₂" long stitch holder
Size 18 tapestry needle

Gauge:
7 sts = 1" in stockinette stitch (knit one row,
  purl one row)

Instructions

Sock (make 2)
Cast on 48 sts.

Divide evenly onto 3 needles, being careful not to
twist sts. Mark beg of rnds.

Cuff:
Rnd 1:
* K2, P2; rep from * around.

Rnd 2:
Rep Rnd 1.

Rnd 3:
* K2 tog leaving sts on left-hand needle; knit first of
these 2 sts; sl sts off left-hand needle; P2; rep from
* 11 times more—12 cables.

Rep Rnds 1 through 3 until cuff measures 5", or
desired length.

Next Two Rnds:
Knit.

Heel:
Sl last 12 sts of last rnd onto free needle; K12 onto same
needle; sl rem 24 sts onto stitch holder for instep. Turn.

HEEL FLAP:
Row 1 (wrong side):
Sl 1 as to purl, purl across. Turn.

Row 2 (right side):
Sl 1 as to knit; * K1, sl 1 as to purl; rep from * 10 times
more; K1.

Rep Rows 1 and 2 until heel flap measures 2³/₄", ending
by working a right side row.

Turning Heel, Gusset, Foot, and Toe Shaping:
Work same as for Basic Sock beg on page 8.

Finishing
See Finishing for Basic Sock on page 9.

TOE TO TOE

Materials:
Berella® Country Garden D.K. sport weight wool yarn,
   3.5 oz (270 yds, 100 g) Lilac Heather #81; 1.75 oz
   (135 yds, 50 g) each, Delphinium #32 and
   Field Flower #19
Size 3 (3.25mm) 7" double-pointed knitting needles,
   or size required for gauge
Size F (3.75mm) crochet hook (optional for picking up sts)
Stitch marker
2¹/₂" long stitch holder
Size 18 tapestry needle

Gauge:
7 sts = 1" in stockinette stitch (knit one row,
   purl one row)

Instructions

Sock (make 2)
With Delphinium, cast on 48 sts.

Divide evenly onto 3 needles, being careful
not to twist sts. Mark beg of rnds.

Rnds 1 through 4:
Purl.

Rnds 5 through 10:
With Lilac Heather, knit.

Rnd 11:
Purl.

Rnds 12 through 17:
Knit.

Rnd 18:
With Field Flower, knit.

Rnds 19 through 22:
With Field Flower, purl.

Rnds 23 through 35:
Rep Rnds 5 through 17.

Rnd 36:
With Delphinium, knit.

Rep Rnds 1 through 17 once.

Heel:
Sl last 12 sts of last rnd onto free needle; K12 onto same
needle; sl rem 24 sts onto stitch holder for instep. Turn.

HEEL FLAP:
Row 1 (wrong side):
With Field Flower, purl. Turn.

Row 2 (right side):
Sl 1 as to knit; * K1, sl 1 as to purl; rep from * 10 times
more; K1. Turn.

Row 3:
Sl 1 as to purl, purl across. Turn.

Rep Rows 2 and 3 until heel flap measures 2³/₄", ending
by working a Row 2.

Turning Heel:
With Field Flower, work same as for Basic Sock beg on
page 8.

Gusset:
With Lilac Heather, work same as for Basic Sock on
page 9.

Foot:
Work same as for Basic Sock on page 9.

Toe Shaping:
Row 1:
With Delphinium, knit.

Continue with toe shaping as for Basic Sock on page 9.

Finishing
See Finishing for Basic Sock on page 9.

STEP RIGHT UP

Materials:

Berella® Country Garden D.K. sport weight wool yarn,
3.5 oz **(**270 yds, 100 g**)** Delphinium #32; 1.75 oz **(**135
yds, 50 g**)** each, Shrimp #14 and Snowdrop #1

Size 3 **(**3.25mm**)** 7" double-pointed knitting needles,
or size required for gauge

Size F **(**3.75mm**)** crochet hook **(**optional for picking
up sts**)**

Stitch marker

2¹/₂" long stitch holder

Size 18 tapestry needle

Gauge:

7 sts = 1" in stockinette stitch **(**knit one row,
purl one row**)**

Instructions

Sock (make 2**)**

With Delphinium, cast on 48 sts.

Divide evenly onto 3 needles, being careful not to
twist sts. Mark beg of rnds.

Ribbing:

Rnd 1:
* K2, P2; rep from ***** 11 times more.

Rnds 2 through 6:
Rep Rnd 1.

Rnd 7:
With Shrimp, knit.

Rnd 8:
Rep Rnd 1.

Rnd 9:
With Snowdrop, knit.

Rnds 10 through 12:
Rep Rnd 1.

Rnds 13 and 14:
Rep Rnds 7 and 8.

Rnd 15:
With Delphinium, knit.

Rnds 16 through 20:
Rep Rnd 1.

Rep Rnds 7 through 20 once, then rep Rnds 7 through
17 once.

Heel:
Continuing with Delphinium, sl last 12 sts of last rnd
onto free needle; K12 onto same needle; sl rem 24 sts
onto stitch holder for instep. Turn.

HEEL FLAP:

Row 1 (wrong side**):**
Sl 1 as to purl, purl across. Turn.

Row 2 (right side**):**
Sl 1 as to knit; ***** K1, sl 1 as to purl; rep from ***** 10 times
more; K1. Turn.

Rep Rows 1 and 2 until heel flap measures 2³/₄", ending
with a right side row.

Turning Heel, Gusset and Foot:
Work same as for Basic Sock beg on page 8, working in following color pattern:

2 rnds Delphinium

2 rnds Shrimp

4 rnds Snowdrop

2 rnds Shrimp

4 rnds Delphinium

Rep color pattern twice more.

Continuing with Delphinium, knit each rnd until foot measures about 2" shorter than desired length of sock (See "Make the correct size..." on page 3).

THIS LITTLE PINKY

Materials:
Berella® Country Garden D.K. sport weight wool yarn,
   3.5 oz (270 yds, 100 g) Scallop Pink #17
Size 3 (3.25mm) 7" double-pointed knitting needles,
   or size required for gauge
Size F (3.75mm) crochet hook (optional for picking
   up sts)
Stitch marker
2¹/₂" stitch holder
Size 18 tapestry needle

Gauge:
7 sts = 1" in stockinette stitch (knit one row,
   purl one row)

Instructions

Sock (make 2)
Cast on 48 sts.

Divide evenly onto 3 needles, being careful not to
twist sts. Mark beg of rnds.

Ribbing:
Rnd 1:
✱ K1, P1; rep from ✱ around.

Rep Rnd 1 until ribbing measures 1¹/₂".

Sl last st on first needle onto second needle; sl first st
on 3rd needle onto second needle. You now have 15 sts
on first needle, 18 sts on 2nd needle, and 15 sts on
3rd needle.

Ankle:
Rnd 1:
✱ YO, sl 1, K2 tog; PSSO; YO, K3; rep from
✱ 7times more.

Rnd 2:
Knit.

Rnds 3 through 8:
Rep Rnds 1 and 2 three times.

Rnd 9:
✱ K3, YO, sl 1, K2 tog; PSSO; YO; rep from
✱ 7 times more.

Rnd 10:
Knit.

Rnds 11 through 16:
Rep Rnds 9 and 10 three times.

Rnds 17 through 24:
Rep Rnds 1 through 8.

Sl first st on 2nd needle to first needle and last st on 2nd
needle to 3rd needle—16 sts on each needle.

Rnds 25 and 26:
Knit.

**Heel, Turning Heel, Gusset, Foot, and Toe
Shaping:**
Work same as for Basic Sock beg on page 8.

Finishing
See Finishing for Basic Sock on page 9.

TOE THE LINE

Materials:
Berella® Country Garden D.K. sport weight wool yarn,
   3.5 oz (270 yds, 100 g) Natural Heather #77
Size 3 (3.25mm) 7" double-pointed knitting needles,
   or size required for gauge
Size F (3.75mm) crochet hook (optional for picking
   up sts)
Stitch marker
2¹/₂" long stitch holder
Size 18 tapestry needle

Gauge:
7 sts = 1" in stockinette stitch (knit one row,
   purl one row)

Special Abbreviation

Slip, Slip, Knit (SSK):
Sl next 2 sts, one at a time, as to knit; insert left-hand
needle through both sts from right to left; K2 tog—
SSK made.

Instructions

Sock (make 2)
Cast on 50 sts.

Being careful not to twist sts, divide sts onto 3 needles,
having 17 sts on first needle, 18 sts on 2nd needle, and
15 sts on 3rd needle. Mark beg of rnds.

Cuff:
Rnd 1:
* P2, K3; rep from * 9 times more.

Rnd 2:
* P2, K1, YO, SSK; rep from * 9 times more.

Rnd 3:
Rep Rnd 1.

Rnd 4:
* P2, K2 tog; YO, K1; rep from * 9 times more.

Rep Rnds 1 through 4 until cuff measures 6".

Next Rnd:
K12, K2 tog; K24, SSK; K10—48 sts. Divide sts evenly
onto 3 needles.

Next Rnd:
Knit.

**Heel, Turning Heel, Gusset, Foot, and Toe
Shaping:**
Work same as for Basic Sock beg on page 8.

Finishing
See Finishing for Basic Sock on page 9.

YOURS, MINE, AND ARGYLES

Materials:
Berella® Country Garden D.K. sport weight wool yarn, 3.5 oz (270 yds, 100 g) Blue Smoke #30; 1.75 oz (135 yds, 50 g) each, Scallop Pink #17 and White Grape #41; 20 yds Snowdrop #1
Size 3 (3.25mm) straight knitting needles, or size required for gauge
Size 3 (3.25mm) 7" double-pointed knitting needles
Size F (3.75mm) crochet hook (optional for picking up sts)
Stitch marker
Three 2¹/₂" long stitch holders
Size 18 tapestry needle

Gauge:
On straight needles, 7 sts = 1" in stockinette stitch (knit one row, purl one row)

Special Abbreviation
Slip, Slip, Knit (SSK):
Sl next 2 sts, one at a time, as to knit; insert left-hand needle through both sts from right to left; K2 tog—SSK made.

Instructions

Sock (make 2)
With straight needles and Blue Smoke, cast on 49 sts.

Ribbing:
Row 1 (right side):
K1; * P1, K1; rep from * across.

Row 2:
P1; * K1, P1; rep from * across.

Rep Rows 1 and 2 until ribbing measures 2".

Ankle and Instep:
Note: Refer to "Working with Charts" on page 6.

Rows 1 through 24:
Work from **Chart A** in stockinette st (knit one row, purl one row).

Row 25:
K12; sl these 12 sts onto one stitch holder; K26 in patt from **Chart A**; sl rem 11 sts onto second stitch holder.

Rows 26 through 47:
Continue working from **Chart A**. At end of Row 47, place these 26 sts onto third stitch holder.

Heel:
Place 11 sts from second stitch holder onto one needle; place 12 sts from first stitch holder onto same needle. Turn.

HEEL FLAP:
Row 1 (wrong side):
With Blue Smoke, sl 1 as to purl, purl 11, inc (purl in front and back of next st); P10—24 sts. Turn.

Row 2 (right side):
Sl 1 as to knit, knit across. Turn.

Row 3:
Sl 1 as to purl, purl across. Turn.

Rep Rows 2 and 3 until heel flap measures 2³/₄", ending by working a Row 2.

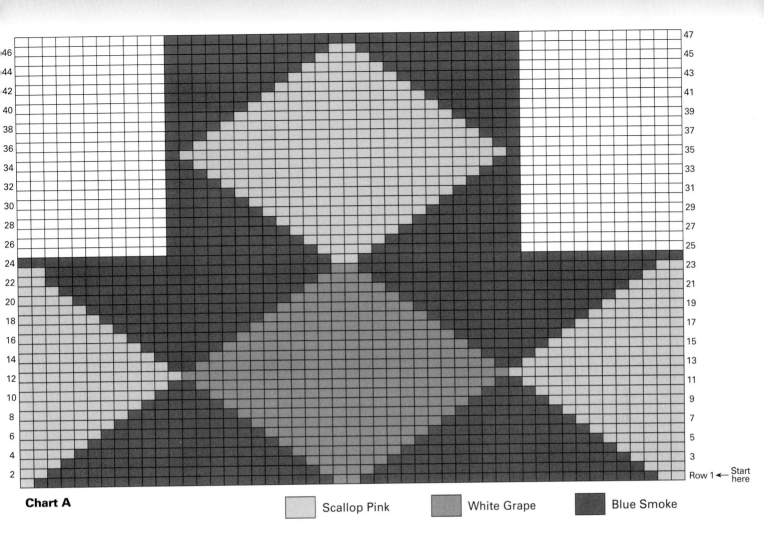

Chart A

■ Scallop Pink   ■ White Grape   ■ Blue Smoke

Turning Heel:

Row 1 (wrong side):
P14, P2 tog; P1. Turn, leaving rem 7 sts unworked.

Row 2 (right side):
Sl 1 as to knit, K5, SSK, K1. Turn, leaving rem 7 sts unworked.

Row 3:
Sl 1 as to purl, P6, P2 tog; P1. Turn, leaving rem 5 sts unworked.

Row 4:
Sl 1 as to knit, K7, SSK, K1. Turn, leaving rem 5 sts unworked.

Row 5:
Sl 1 as to purl, P8, P2 tog; P1. Turn, leaving rem 3 sts unworked.

Row 6:
Sl 1 as to knit, K9, SSK, K1. Turn, leaving rem 3 sts unworked.

Row 7:
Sl 1 as to purl, P10, P2 tog; P1. Turn, leaving rem st unworked.

Row 8:
Sl 1 as to knit, K11, SSK, K1. Turn, leaving rem st unworked.

Row 9:
Sl 1 as to purl, P12, P2 tog. Turn.

Row 10:
Sl 1 as to knit, K12, SSK—14 sts. Cut Blue Smoke.

Gusset:
Note: Gusset is worked back and forth in rows on double-pointed needles. If using crochet hook to pick up sts, it is necessary to slip them onto a double-pointed needle.

With right side of heel flap facing you, with Blue Smoke and crochet hook (or double-pointed needle), pick up 13 sts along right side of heel flap; knit 14 heel sts onto second double-pointed needle, with crochet hook (or third double-pointed needle), pick up 13 sts along left side of heel flap—40 sts. Turn.

Row 1 (wrong side):
With Blue Smoke, purl.

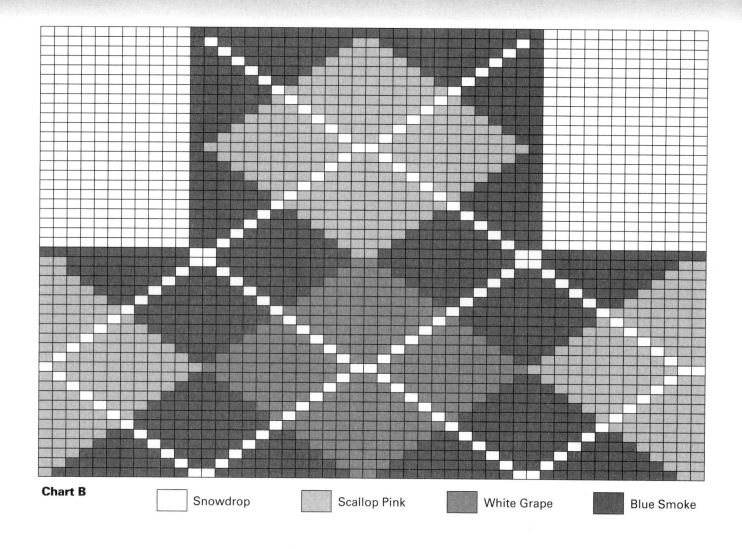

Chart B

☐ Snowdrop   ▨ Scallop Pink   ▨ White Grape   ■ Blue Smoke

Row 2:
K1, SSK; knit to last 3 sts on third needle; K2 tog; K1—38 sts.

Rows 3 through 18:
Rep Rows 1 and 2 eight times. At end of Row 18—22 sts.

Rows 19 through 23:
Work even in stockinette stitch. Turn. Cut Blue Smoke.

Gusset should measure same length as instep.

Sl first 7 sts from second needle onto end of first needle; sl rem 7 sts from second needle onto beg of third needle; sl instep sts from stitch holder onto free needle; sl one st onto first needle and one st from opposite end onto third needle. You should have 24 instep sts on one needle, and 12 sts each on 2 needles.

Foot:
Note: Foot is worked in rnds. Join Blue Smoke in first st at center of heel. Mark beg of rnds.

Rnd 1:
On first needle, K12; on second needle, K24; on third needle, K12.

Work even until foot measures about 2" shorter than desired length of sock (See "Make the correct size..." on page 3).

Toe Shaping:
Work same as for Basic Sock beg on page 8.

Finishing
Step 1:
With tapestry needle, weave toe together (see Special Techniques on page 6). Weave in all ends.

Step 2:
With white, and referring to **Chart B**, work diagonal lines in duplicate st (see Special Techniques beginning on page 6).

Step 3:
Turn sock inside out. With right sides together, and carefully matching stitches, sew instep and gusset seam; sew back heel seam.